CULINARY ROOTS

Food From the Soul of a People

Published by Pecan Tree Publishing, December 2008

Hollywood, FL

www.pecantreepress.com

This book or parts thereof may not be reproduced in any form, stored in a retrieval system, or transmitted in any form by any means – electronic, mechanical, photocopy, recording, or otherwise – without prior written permission of the publisher, author or legal representative of both parties, except as provided by United States of America copyright law.

Copyright © 2008 Brenda L. Jackson

Library of Congress Control Number: 2009921045

All rights reserved.

ISBN-13: 978-0-9821114-1-3

ISBN-10: 0-9821114-1-3

CULINARY ROOTS

Food From the Soul of a People

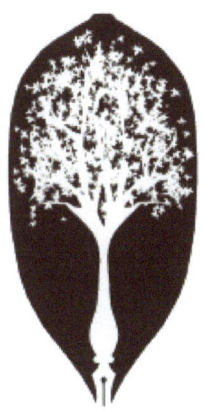

Brenda L. Jackson

Pecan Tree Publishing

PO Box 470697, Miami, Fl 33247

877-207-2442 www.pecantreepress.com

info@pecantreepress.com

Culinary Roots

Home-style southern cooking with delicate gourmet twists; peppered with stories that carried us from generation to generation

Brenda L. Jackson

Photography:
Ada Stevens

Craig Stafford (Pgs 35, 37 and 47)

Book Cover and Layout:
Angelica Velez

Tablescape Design (Cover):
Laura Benitez

In memory of my father and to my mother
Orlando and Florida Jackson
Who not only taught me, but showed me the importance of
family

&

To my best friend and sweetheart
Pete Billings
Who has blessed my life with his love, wisdom and support

Acknowledgments

I am grateful for all the experiences in my life as they have brought me to this point. There are many people I have encountered who have created moments in my life that will never be forgotten. To the following I say thank you:

E. Claudette Freeman, publisher and editor of Pecan Tree Publishing, whose work and support went beyond the call of duty in sampling every recipe in this book, excluding the crab bisque due to her food allergies.

Bishop Victor T. Curry, my pastor and father in ministry, for the empowerment teachings and generosity of resources in providing visibility of the book.

Vernita Williams, my mentor and life coach, for being an example of discipline in making the usage of time purposeful and profitable.

To the Reid and Jackson families, thank you for a strong foundation that continues to sustain as generations are born and develop. I am thankful for the blessing of family and the wisdom that is passed through the years.

Friends of old and friends of new, your support and unconditional love never cease to amaze me.

Most important, I am thankful to God for another door of opportunity.

Culinary Roots

Brenda L. Jackson

Foreword
Food that Sustains

Understanding that God ordained family and placed them in a garden, and within this setting everything to sustain life was within their reach. Today in a family every gift to sustain life is there. There is uniqueness and individuality in each of us. Recipes for wholesomeness and richness - the same is true when we think of plants, fruits, nuts, etc. Someone somewhere is forever putting together ingredients that fuel our life's existence. We love foods. There is a saying "you are what you eat." Coming from a large family and remembering that my mom would take one chicken and fix it in a way that all of us were full. There were 13 of us in the family filled from one chicken. Oh yes, there were other things, like rice, potatoes, vegetables that went along as side dishes. Little became much when it was placed in the hand of our mom and grand mom, Georgia Elizabeth.

We were blessed to live on a farm where we raised and grew the things we ate which probably helps our account for being such robust and healthy people. We grew things like greens, peas, bean, cane, peanuts, corn, okra, tomatoes, and potatoes and also raised animals – cows, hogs, chickens and goats. We had nut trees and fruit trees. You name it, it was on our farm.

Physically we were fit. We had to attend to the farm and animals, and this afforded us all the physical exercise we needed. With the death of our father, John Henry, mom sold the farm and moved to the city of Gainesville, Florida. Most of her children were grown and gone at that time and she felt the need to not live so far out. Then mom's grandchildren came along- my nieces and nephews. I was the youngest of the 13 and I loved my nieces and nephews. I had the opportunity to be aunt, big sister and also the big family I was used to continued with their presence.

Brenda, the elder daughter of my sister, Florida Mae was always special and definitely stood out from the crowd. I remember Brenda was always the one with an inquisitive mind and a love for food and family. It is no surprise then that she would put together a book --- Culinary Roots – that honors both things. Spending time at our family house and individual homes - food was a pastime, a hobby we all shared and on it was always so, so good. Meatloaf, chicken and rice, jelly cakes – collard greens were foods we loved. I hope this book brings back your own precious memories and brings your family back to the table - together for food for the body and food that sustains.

Wilma Reid Camps

THE WHO, WHY & HOW - ME

I am so excited about this cookbook. Cooking is one of my passions, so a cookbook seems an obvious choice as I launch my literary career. Cooking relaxes me and grocery shopping, (while a chore for some) is a time of discovery for me. Looking at all the variety of food items in the stores, allows my mind to wonder. Wonder it does! With every aisle I think - what would taste good with what?

Culinary Roots provides what I believe is a wonderful glimpse into the memories and moments of my family and food has always been and is still an integral part of our living. Food of course sustains life, but in my family it was the catalyst for frequent gatherings of the minds; a time for individual lives to be discussed and opinions on the same exchanged.

As I introduce you to me, let me shake the family tree and reveal the weird stuff right off the bat. My parents are Orlando and Florida Jackson. Yes the names are real! Their meeting was divine intervention. My daddy, born in Ft. Valley, Georgia, moved to Miami in his adult years. My mama, Florida Mae Victoria Reid, born in Ellisville, Florida, later moved to Gainesville, Florida. The two met at a church meeting. My daddy being enamored with my mama would travel the 400 miles necessary to spend time with her. My daddy's pastor was curious as to why my father would travel so far to see a woman when there were plenty of single women in his own church. My daddy's reply to the pastor was that the women at his church in Miami were not as pretty as Miss Florida Reid...

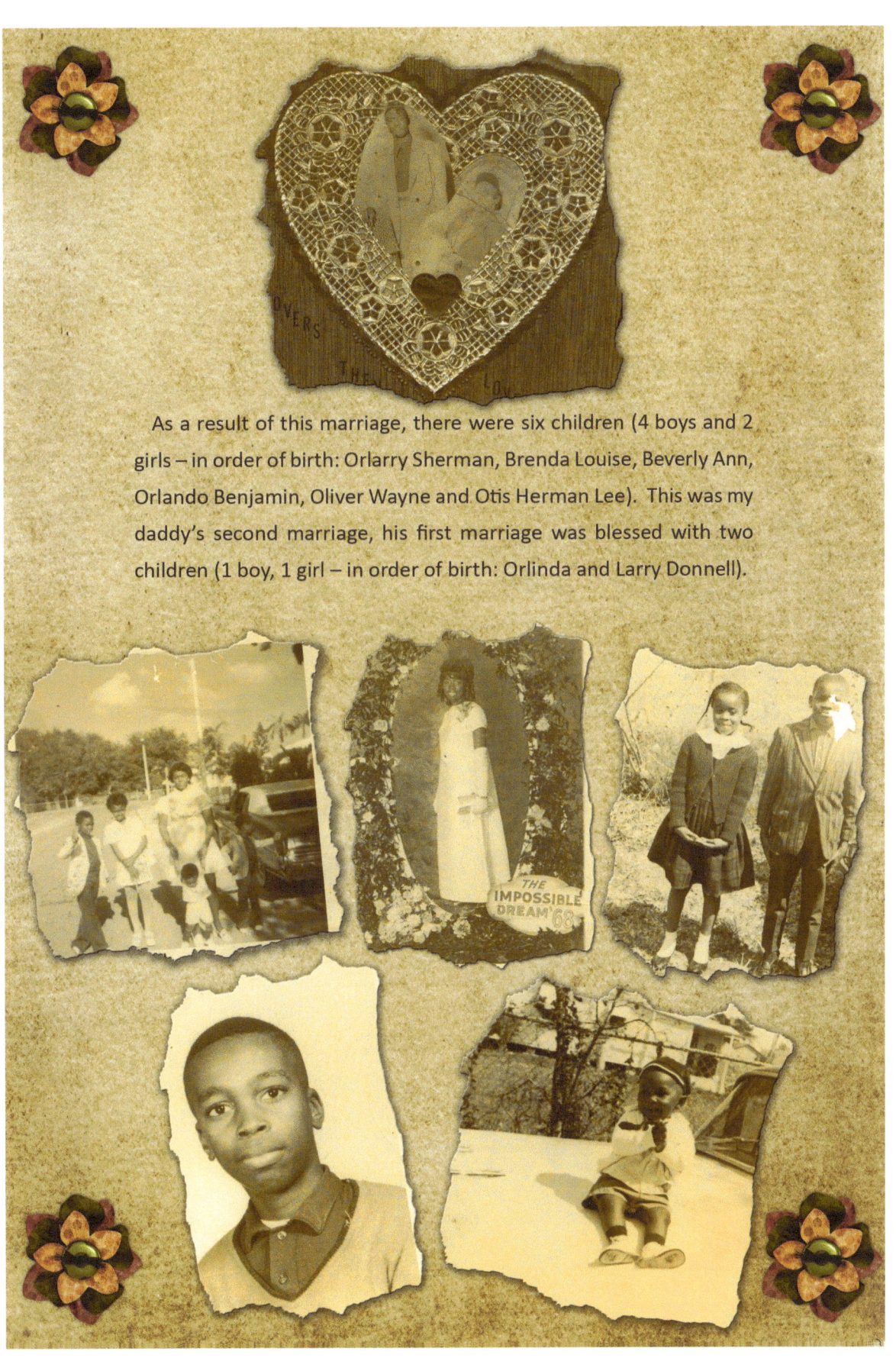

As a result of this marriage, there were six children (4 boys and 2 girls – in order of birth: Orlarry Sherman, Brenda Louise, Beverly Ann, Orlando Benjamin, Oliver Wayne and Otis Herman Lee). This was my daddy's second marriage, his first marriage was blessed with two children (1 boy, 1 girl – in order of birth: Orlinda and Larry Donnell).

Another weird leaf from the family tree is that my mother is a twin. Her twin sister's name is Georgia Mae Elizabeth. Yes, again the names are real and stop laughing! Aunt Georgia, the sister-in-law of Orlando Jackson, lives – are you ready for this – in Orlando, Florida! I promise I am not making this stuff up! I went through many episodes of being called a liar by teachers, friends, co-workers, etc. when relaying my family-names story.

As I eluded to earlier, I love to cook and since my parents were "old school", and I was the oldest girl in the house, I not only needed to know how to cook – I had to cook. My mama taught me how to cook from a basic perspective. The adventurous side of food and cooking came from my father. Daddy was a cook on the train. He rode the Miami to Chicago route along with his father Herman Lee Jackson. Daddy was used to cooking in large portions for passengers and crew; so with six kids in the house he was already prepared to feed a multitude. My ranking in the family, second oldest child/oldest daughter, meant I had to help with the smaller kids. One of my duties was to assist with mealtime. I was the preparer of the plates.

The phrase you would often hear when stomachs became really hungry was - "Bren fix my eat." If we had spaghetti, then it was "Bren fix my schetto." Yes – schetto – don't ask. Speaking of spaghetti, my mama had her own version of spaghetti and meatballs. The meatballs were just ground beef, seasoned, shaped like a hamburger, fried and then added to the spaghetti and tomato sauce. This was the only spaghetti I knew. I later learned other variations and sauces and so I became the new chef on spaghetti days.

I ventured off into cooking before I finished taking a look at the rest of the family tree. My maternal grandparents, Henry and Georgia, knew each other since they were nine years old. Henry and his brother Ed saw Georgia Elizabeth and her sister, Clennie Victoria and Ed decided that he and Henry would marry them. This all at the ripe old age of nine. Henry was to marry Georgia and Ed was to marry Clennie. Both unions came true. My grandparents were married in 1916. Their union produced 18 children, 5 died at childbirth. The remaining 13 lived to full adulthood. At present there are two brothers and four sisters surviving. My family is implanted with a line of preachers/ministers, beginning with my grandfather and that continues even with me.

Summertime meant the grandchildren were gathering in Gainesville, Florida. Those summer days were wonderful, mainly because we knew we would have the chance to taste all that grandmother would create. Food and my grandmother were synonymous. You knew there would always be something good to eat in her house. Grandmother had an old buffet which was always covered with cakes and pies: jelly cakes, 7-up pound cakes, chocolate cakes, sweet potato pies and pecan pies.

Feeding large groups of people was never a problem in my family. You see my mama had six kids and my Aunt Georgia, had six kids. Many times we would all visit grandmother's home at the same time. My grandmother would fix a large pot of grits with butter and all of us would line up for breakfast. When my grandmother cooked, it was always from scratch and the vegetables were always fresh. Every meal required much preparation. This typically meant a trip to the farmer's market and then time on the porch shelling peas and snapping beans. What stories would be shared during those times. With 13 children in the family, you know there were a lot of things we could and did get into; throughout this book I will share some of those family moments with you. (Don't laugh too hard at what we've done.)

One year my Uncle Earl took us to the first family house in Ellisville, Florida. Just to see this small house, not more than 900-1,000 square feet amazed me; especially considering the size of the family that had been raised there. Some of the wood floors were still in good condition. I was taken back in time and could almost see my mama as a child, living without the cares of raising her own children.

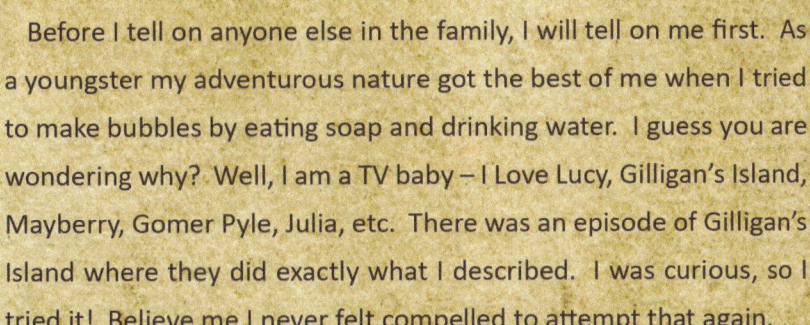

Before I tell on anyone else in the family, I will tell on me first. As a youngster my adventurous nature got the best of me when I tried to make bubbles by eating soap and drinking water. I guess you are wondering why? Well, I am a TV baby – I Love Lucy, Gilligan's Island, Mayberry, Gomer Pyle, Julia, etc. There was an episode of Gilligan's Island where they did exactly what I described. I was curious, so I tried it! Believe me I never felt compelled to attempt that again.

As mentioned earlier, my cooking style is two-fold: know how and the willingness to experiment. Some of the ingredients used in my recipes may seem a little unusual. I enjoy the discovery of flavors and how they work with other flavors. My grocery shopping, although seemingly exaggerated, is not unlike that of an anthropologist or any other explorer. Taking the things I like to eat or have experienced feeds my intrigue with food. I love watching cooking shows and assessing their use of ingredients, preparation and presentation. My good friend Roz always teases me and believes I could watch the shows all day. She is, of course, correct.

Back to flavors or ingredients – one of the favorite is Cilantro. Cilantro is used a lot in Mexican/Southwestern cooking. I have used both the dried and fresh version. For my avocado salad, I add fresh cilantro because it brightens up all the flavors of the lime, fresh tomatoes and Bermuda onions. The dry variety I use in my collard greens, for a brightening of flavors. My thought process is usually: why not – what if I– I wonder if I use and so on. The old adage of "nothing beats a failure, but a try" pushes my openness to experiment in my cooking.

My most recent discovery is Panko (Japanese Bread Flakes). Again I am an avid cooking show fan.

In my opinion, The Iron Chef (original and America) shows the most diverse dishes and thus diverse ingredients. Panko was used many times in the battles, so I thought why not on my fried chicken.

Growing up on southern foods will always be a mainstay of my cooking journey. Both my parents were farmers. They knew how to work the soil, milk cows, and pluck chickens and prepare your routine farm animals for a family meal. Aah, but there were the normal oddities as well, opossum, raccoons, squirrel and different types of birds. I call them normal oddities, because they were normal in the South, but considered odd in other parts of the country. My dad was a hunter and a fisherman, so I never was naïve about how food got to the plate. I have seen chickens killed, boiled and plucked.

Even though our home was in the city (Miami, Florida) we definitely experienced some parts of the farm life. We had our own garden, where we grew collards, turnips, mustards, tomatoes, cabbage, okra and peas. Daddy would build traps to place in the woods to catch opossums and raccoons. He went rabbit hunting as well. One time he even caught a bobcat. I found it in our deep freezer. I know we never ate it, but maybe we did and weren't told. There were many times I would go into the kitchen to find a hog's head on the dining room table or half of the hog laying on newspapers in the dining room.

I even learned to gut and clean fish and turtle. This was something I wanted to learn. It intrigued me to see the unusual when it came to food. My dad's precision with the knife and knowing what the parts of the turtle and fish were was like watching cooks at a Japanese restaurant. He would keep the fish roe (fish eggs) and cook that as well. I didn't like eating that part though. I have eaten frog legs, rabbit, bird and other things I probably don't want to know about.

My daddy was a great cook. He loved spicy foods, so most of what he made would have a little kick to it. His turtle stew always brought his friends around. If they knew he was making this dish, they would come two hours early and sit and wait for it. I loved my turtle fried and smothered over white rice. That was good eating.

My siblings and I were always happy when daddy would cook a steak. Since daddy did everything in large portions, we knew even though he only would cook one steak that it would be so large that he would never finish it himself. We were like vultures circling a dead corpse waiting for daddy to reach satisfaction with his meal and place the plate on the stove. We would then wait a decent period of time before starting our mission of who would conquer the prize. My daddy's steak was the best. Daddy would always get t-bone. He loved those. To best describe it, he would season the meat with just salt and pepper, but he would pan sear it in butter and then let it slow cook adding just a little water to finish. Oh my sweet Lord that was good. When we heard the sizzle we knew there was joy to be had.

I came to the discovery that creativity in preparation and eye appeal can draw a hesitant palate to become quite intrigued. It pleases me when someone has never had a certain dish and my cooking is their first experience and they love it. I have had many protestors make the adamant declaration – "I don't like macaroni and cheese" – yet they are drawn into tasting my recipe for it and love it. That is the ultimate compliment for me.

Throughout this book are family photos from grandparents to grandchildren. There was no way I could fit everyone in because the book would be too big and the publisher would have had to increase the purchase price. Aren't' you glad I didn't?

I hope you slowly tour the book, looking at the photos, reading the humorous anecdotes and of course savor the recipes.

I long for our families to go back to the time of eating at one table for a meal. A family having a conversation which births laughter, commentary, questions or deep thought. We have lost the art of conversation. Those times on my grandmother's porch, listening to the stories being shared is a rich memory for me in my present adulthood.

I want to share a part of that richness through this cookbook entitled Culinary Roots. Thank you for being a guest in my kitchen and at the family table.

Brenda L. Jackson

Family Memories

Family Memories

BE BLESSED

The proudest moment in the life of any parent manifests as we witness the maturation and evolution of our children. Brenda has produced a wonderful collection of traditions both in tales and tempting treats. With flair that is uniquely hers, she provides an interesting and informative indulgence for the delight of her readers. As her Pastor and spiritual father I am, yet again, encouraged by her creativity and the marvelous use of her many gifts and talents.

My prayer is that the God and Father of our Lord Jesus Christ, who delights in his children, will bless this work; the working of the gift that He placed in Brenda. I invoke His manifold blessings of joy and hospitality to each one of you. May the love of our Lord and the sweet communion of the Holy Spirit fill your homes as you prepare, serve and celebrate. I pray your continued blessings of every good and perfect gift. May your family and friends be overtaken by the sumptuous and comforting dishes that you will assuredly enjoy!

God bless you,
Bishop Victor T. Curry, D. Min., D. Div.
Senior Pastor/Teacher
New Birth Baptist Church Cathedral of Faith International
Miami, Florida

TABLE OF CONTENTS

Baked sweet potato fries	*2*
Barbecue bacon turkey meatloaf	*3*
BBQ pigs' feet	*4*
Broccoli cheese casserole	*5*
Collard greens and tomatoes	*9*
Cornbread casserole	*13*
Honey key lime chicken wings	*14*
Layered salad	*16*
Lemon pepper panko crusted fried chicken	*18*
Macaroni and cheese	*22*
Mashed potato salad	*24*
Mojito fruit salad	*25*
Quick tomato crab bisque w/croutons	*29*
Red beans and rice	*31*
Salad treasure	*35*
Sausage bacon bites	*37*
Sausage stew	*39*
Smothered catfish	*41*
Steamed tilapia w/sundried tomatoes and spinach	*44*
Stewed oxtails	*45*
Sweet and spicy tuna salad	*47*
Teriyaki BBQ turkey wings	*51*
Vegetable medley	*54*
Wasabi spinach mashed potatoes	*56*

Memories

Baked Sweet Potato Fries

4 Medium Sweet Potatoes
Black Pepper
Cinnamon
Olive Oil

- Cut potatoes julienne style; rinse potatoes and blot with a paper towel; season potatoes with black pepper and cinnamon to taste; pour olive oil on potatoes; gently toss with your fingers to ensure all the fries are coated.

- Place fries in large shallow baking pan or cookie sheet (coated with cooking spray).

- Preheat oven to 400 degrees and bake for 45-50 minutes.

Barbecue Bacon Turkey Meatloaf

1 green bell pepper chopped
1 clove of garlic chopped
3 tbsp olive oil
2 lbs ground turkey
1 pkg onion soup mix
2 eggs

2 eggs
1½ cup bread crumbs plain
¼ cup barbecue sauce
1 tsp salt
1 tsp pepper
6 thinly sliced bacon strips

- Sauté garlic and pepper in olive oil until peppers are tender.

- In bowl mix thoroughly ground turkey, onion soup mix, sautéed garlic and bell pepper, eggs, bread crumbs, barbecue sauce, salt, pepper.

- On a sheet of parchment paper in a lattice formation layout the bacon. Take ground turkey mixture and place on top of bacon, as you fold parchment paper to wrap mixture shape into a loaf.

- Place in shallow pan and bake at 350 degrees for 1 hour.

- When done, let rest for 20 minutes. Flip so that bacon shows on top. Brush with barbecue sauce and broil on low until bacon is crisp and sauce is baked in.

CULINARY ROOTS — 3 — **BRENDA L. JACKSON**

BBQ Pigs' Feet

2-3 lbs pigs' feet (have butcher chop, if not already)

1 tbsp minced garlic

1 tbsp red pepper flakes

½ cup vinegar

1 bottle barbecue sauce

- Rinse pigs' feet and place in large pot covering with water; add in garlic, red pepper flakes and vinegar. Boil for 40-50 minutes or until tender. Drain pig feet and place in baking pan, pouring ½ bottle barbecue sauce on pig feet.

- Preheat oven to 350, baking for 20 minutes; add remaining sauce and broil for 10 minutes allowing sauce to bake into the skin and crackle. Remember to monitor when on broil as sugar in sauce can burn quickly.

Broccoli Cheese Casserole

CULINARY ROOTS — 5 — **BRENDA L. JACKSON**

Broccoli Cheese Casserole

2 16 oz bags frozen broccoli
1 ½ sticks butter
1 ½ tbsp flour
1 tsp black pepper
1 tsp kosher salt
1 tsp garlic powder
1 cup evaporated milk
12 oz bag of shredded cheddar cheese
Complete seasoning to taste
½ bag crushed cheese crackers

- Rinse broccoli and set aside in baking dish, allowing to thaw to room temperature. In a small sauce pan melt ½ stick butter, adding flour, black pepper, kosher salt and garlic powder. Stir gently incorporating flour evenly. This is your roux for your cheese sauce. Add evaporated milk. Add shredded cheese in parts stir each time over a low medium heat until you acquire a thickening in the cheese sauce.

- Place broccoli in casserole dish and sprinkle complete seasonings; gently incorporate seasoning throughout the broccoli; pour cheese sauce, spreading to cover broccoli.

Topping:
Pour ½ bag of cheese crackers in bowl or bag and crush; melt 1 stick of butter in sauce pan; add crackers, stirring until crackers have absorbed the butter. Pour over broccoli and cheese evenly; add remaining shredded cheese on top.
Preheat oven to 350 degrees. Bake for 10-20 minutes until cheese and crackers are golden brown.

Family Memories

My Aunt Mildred was the tattle-tale of the family. Whatever mischief the brothers and sisters got into, Mildred would be the first to break to their parents to tell what occurred in their absence. In one instance the tables were turned on my aunt when my mama found some poems Mildred was writing to a boy in school in her notebook. Mama showed it to my grandmother. It read:

Roses are red

Violets are blue

Sugar is sweet, but not like you.

True as the grass grows around the stump

You are my darling sugar lump.

You can walk around the mountain

And fall in the deep blue sea

But baby you ain't did no falling

'Til you fell in love with me.

The boy never got a chance to receive it though because my grandmother destroyed my aunt's poetic masterpiece.

MEMORIES

Collard Greens And Tomatoes

CULINARY ROOTS — 9 — **BRENDA L. JACKSON**

Collard Greens and Tomatoes

2 bags already cleaned and cut collard greens
1 can stewed tomatoes
1 jar medium spicy salsa
2 packets chicken bouillon
4-5 dashes of hot sauce
3 scotch bonnet peppers
½ cup sugar
2 tbsp balsamic vinegar
½ lb of smoked turkey wings
or 1 drumstick (cut-up)
Complete seasoning
Black pepper to taste
1 tbsp cilantro
½ tsp red pepper flakes

- Wash greens. In large pot (4 quart) place smoked turkey cover with water; boil until fork tender. Add 1st bag of greens and dry seasonings. As greens cook down add 2nd bag. Once greens have cooked down add stewed tomatoes, salsa, scotch bonnet peppers and seasonings.

- Let slow cook for 2-3 hours or until greens are tender.

- If you like heat, leave scotch bonnets in. If not remove after peppers have collapsed.

Culinary Roots — Brenda L. Jackson

A Collard Green Warning
(I Mean Sidebar)

The death of a loved one is a sad occasion. I have noticed that even under these circumstances you can find laughter. This year my best friend Roz Kinsey's dad died. As is customary with funerals, we bring food to the family home to ensure that the bereaved has something prepared and ready to sustain their physical strength. Something they should not worry about. Also the food is an extension and demonstration of your love for that family in their time of sadness.

During one of my visits I asked Roz - what I could cook for the wake. She and her friend/co-worker Cathy Clarke said almost simultaneously collard greens. Well I was more than happy to oblige. When preparing my greens I like to give them a bit of a kick. This entails, red pepper flakes and scotch bonnet peppers (a Jamaican pepper that is EXTREMELY hot).   In the cooking I let the peppers explode. As you may or may not know the heat of a pepper is in the seed not the flesh. You can see where this is going!

I took the greens over to the house and during the following week, I called to ask if people enjoyed the greens. I am told that there were tears, facial sweats and various vocal noises made. These sounds, I'm told, had nothing to do with the loss of a loved one, but the heat of the greens.   With every tear, drop of sweat or moan of satisfaction, the consensus was - "Boy these greens hot, but give me some more!" While I did not mean to create such an eruption with the dish, I am glad for their distraction if only for a moment.

Culinary Roots 12 Brenda L. Jackson

Cornbread Casserole

- 2 boxes cornbread mix
- ½ medium green bell pepper (chopped)
- ½ medium red bell pepper (chopped)
- 1 medium onion
- 16 oz sour cream
- 1 can creamed style corn
- 2 eggs
- 1 stick butter (melted)
- 16 oz pkg breakfast sausage
- Pinch of red pepper flakes
- 1 tbsp complete seasonings
- 1 tsp black pepper
- 1 tbsp minced garlic
- 1 tbsp olive oil

- Chop onion and peppers. In a fry pan sauté minced garlic, onion and peppers in olive oil. When the vegetables are almost tender add breakfast sausage. Use a fork to scramble sausage. Cook until sausage has browned. Drain meat and vegetable mixture.

- In a bowl add cornbread mix, sour cream, creamed style corn, seasonings, 2 eggs and melted butter. Fold in sausage mixture.

- Spray 13x9x2 pan with cooking spray. Pour mixture in pan and bake for 30-40 minutes in 350 degree oven, until golden brown.

- For the non-pork eaters, use ground turkey in place of the sausage, seasoning the ground turkey with sage, fennel seed, thyme, garlic powder, salt and pepper gives it a sausage flavor.

Honey Key Lime Chicken Wings

Culinary Roots 14 Brenda L. Jackson

Honey Key Lime Chicken Wings

2-3 lbs chicken wings

4 key limes

1 cup natural honey

Grill seasoning to taste

Kosher salt to taste

- Wash chicken thoroughly. Place wings in a plastic storage bag; squeeze limes onto the chicken; also place limes in the bag; add seasoning. Let chicken marinate for 30 minutes or overnight. The longer, the better.

- Pour wings along with marinade mixture in a large baking pan, spreading the wings out evenly. Cover with foil.

- Preheat oven to 350 and bake for 1 hour or until tender. Remove foil, pour honey on wings and bake uncovered for 10 minutes; broil on low for another 10 minutes until honey has caramelized and skin is slightly crispy on the wings.

Layered Salad

Layered Salad

1 salad bag – Romaine and Radicchio (chopped)

3 stalks of celery – chopped

1 red bell pepper – chopped

1 green bell pepper – chopped

1 Bermuda onion – chopped

1 bag frozen corn

1 jar whipped salad dressing or any thick dressing you like

Sprinkle of garlic powder w/parsley

1 bag shredded cheddar cheese

1 jar or bag of real bacon bits

- Chop all the vegetables including the salad bag. I know the salad is already prepared for eating, but chopping it again, gives a better look and it goes further.

- Next, in a glass bowl layer the ingredients in the order as listed.

- The best thing about this salad is - you make it yours. Add beans, tomatoes, shrimp, and grill chicken, whatever. Be creative!

- This salad makes a great party contribution both in taste and color.

Culinary Roots — **Brenda L. Jackson**

Lemon Pepper Panko Crusted Fried Chicken

Culinary Roots — Brenda L. Jackson

Lemon Pepper Panko Crusted Fried Chicken

2 lbs boneless chicken breast
Mojo marinade as needed
2 eggs
2 tablespoon water
Flour
Lemon pepper seasoning salt to taste
1 fresh lemon
Panko (Japanese Bread Flakes)

- Rinse chicken well. If the breasts are thick, split in half and pound out thickness. This is beneficial to ensure your chicken cooks thoroughly when using a batter coating.

- Marinade chicken breast in Mojo for 1 hour or overnight if you prefer. Sprinkle with lemon pepper seasoning salt and half of a fresh lemon.

- Prepare three dipping/dredging stations: flour, egg mixture (2 eggs and 2 tablespoons water); and Panko flakes.

- Lightly dredge chicken in flour; coat with egg mixture; pressed flakes onto chicken. Continue in this order until all of the chicken is coated.

- Fry in oil until golden brown.

Family Memories

Food, and the preparation of the same, sometimes became a dangerous thing for me. There are two incident that ring clear in my mind.

Brenda L. Jackson dangerous culinary encounter #1. Remember the old pressure cookers? I certainly do! One day my mom decided to cook a hen for dinner and the pressure cooker was her method of choice. I was 15 or so at the time and being on the phone was my favorite pastime; one that especially irritated my mom on that particular day. I'm sitting in the dining room enjoying my conversation, when I decided to act like I was helping. In my mind, this would keep my mom quiet about the fact that I was STILL on the phone. I sashayed my hips to the stove, yacking away and proceeded to open that pressure cooker. It all happened in seconds. The hen flew to the ceiling (sticking!). The steam hit my face full force, causing burns and cutting my eyelid. I screamed, my mama ran into the kitchen and we then proceeded to the hospital emergency room.

Brenda L. Jackson's dangerous culinary encounter #2. This caper included my cousins from my dad's side of the family. The victims: I, Lorraine, Gail, Beverly (my sister), Paula, Larry (my brother), Harold, Barbara, and I think Jerry. My Aunt Donnie Lee (my dad's sister), had a large pepper bush in her backyard. There was a detached garage that we would play in. We were playing restaurant and the special for the day was peppers. We started washing the peppers, preparing plates and serving. We were having a good time until we all made the fatal mistake of opening the peppers and then touching our faces with pepper stained fingers. The burn, the burn, oh God the burn – eyes, mouth. We were on fire. We had to wait until the sting just wore off.

FAMILY MEMORIES

Macaroni and Cheese

Macaroni and Cheese

16 oz elbow macaroni or penne pasta
1 stick butter
3 tbsp flour
1 tbsp complete seasoning
1 can evaporated milk
8 oz shredded sharp cheddar cheese
8 oz shredded mild cheese
8 oz shredded four cheese Mexican style blend
 (Monterey jack, cheddar, queso blanco and asadero cheeses)
1 can cream of chicken soup
1 tsp pepper
1 1l/2 cup bread crumbs seasoned (topping)

Cheese Sauce:

In a sauce pan melt butter; add flour; complete seasoning; pepper and cream of chicken soup; stirring slowly; add evaporated milk, allowing it to slowly warm. Gently add 2 ½ bags of cheese in parts stirring slowly. Continue to stir allowing cheese to melt.

Follow package directions for cooking pasta. Spray baking dish with non-stick cooking spray and pour in pasta.

- Once cheese sauce is at a thick consistency and easily pourable, fold in with pasta incorporating the cheese sauce throughout.

- Sprinkle remaining cheese and bread crumbs on top with 4-6 pats of butter to make the bread crumbs golden brown.

- Bake at 350 degrees for 30 minutes, until cheese and bread crumb topping is golden brown.

CULINARY ROOTS 23 **BRENDA L. JACKSON**

Mashed Potato Salad

9 medium russet potatoes
4 boiled eggs
1 ½ cup whipped salad dressing
1 tbsp kosher salt
½ tsp white pepper
½ tsp black pepper
1 tsp garlic powder
2 tbsp sugar
½ cup ranch dressing

Peel potatoes and boil in salted water until potatoes are tender then drain. Mash potatoes to a grainy consistency. Make sure to add these items while potatoes are still hot: whipped salad dressing, ranch dressing, salt, white pepper, black pepper, garlic powder, sugar. Gently fold in all ingredients reaching your desired smoothness of the mixture.

Place in a bowl. Garnish with sliced eggs, paprika and chives.

Refrigerate for at least 1 hour before serving.

Mojito Fruit Salad

Culinary Roots 25 **Brenda L. Jackson**

Mojito Fruit Salad

2 lb fruit salad bowl from the market
1 1/3 cup rum (flavored, white)
2 tbsp fresh mint – finely chopped
1 lime

- Combine rum, mint, lime juice first. Pour mixture over fruit salad. Gently incorporate to coat all of the fruit.

- Cover and refrigerated for 1 hour. Garnish with a sprig of mint.

Quick Tomato Crab Bisque w/Croutons

Quick Tomato Crab Bisque w/ Croutons

1 16 oz fresh crabmeat (claw)

1 can cream of celery soup

1 can New England clam chowder

1 6 oz can tomato paste

Half and half (measure in soup can)

Pepper, garlic powder

and crushed red peppers to taste

1 tbsp white wine

2 caps of sherry

Croutons

- 6 slices of bread (wheat, white, etc.)
  Olive oil
  Celery seed

- Chop bread into ½ inch cubes; place on cookie sheet (coated with cooking spray); sprinkle with olive oil and celery seed.

- Preheat oven to 350 degrees. Bake until bread is browned.

- Combine all ingredients in medium size sauce pan; slowly bring to a boil; pour mixture in blender and pulse until you have a smooth consistency. If you have hand blender all the better – blend it in the pot. Add more sherry for a thinner consistency.

- Allow to simmer for 5-10 minutes. Serve with homemade celery bread croutons.

Red Beans and Rice

Red Beans and Rice

14 oz bag dry red kidney beans
½ lb smoked turkey
1 tsp cilantro
1 tbsp minced garlic
1 tbsp white pepper
1 tbsp black pepper
2 lbs Cajun sausage
1/3 cup evaporated milk
2 pkts chicken bouillon
2 tsp Cajun seasoning

- Soak beans in a bowl of water for 30 minutes.

- In a 3 quart pot cover smoked turkey with water and cook until meat is slightly tender. Drain soaked beans and add to smoked turkey. Add dry seasonings and sliced sausage. Slow cook on medium heat for 1 hour. Then add ½ cup evaporated milk and simmer for another 10-20 minutes.

- Serve with parboiled rice or cornbread.

Family Memories

Food and entertaining are synonymous in my adult years. There was a season where my cousin Lorraine and I were constantly preparing for one party or another. The occasions varied, but food, drink and music were our key elements for a great time. During one of these times of preparation, Lorraine and her sisters - Paula, Helen and I took a late night/early morning (12:00 a.m.) trip to the store to purchase food for a party.

Upon entering the store, I grabbed a shopping cart and we headed towards the produce department. Lorraine decided we would need another cart and so she went back to retrieve it. Now Helen and Paula are standing at the side of my cart facing the direction of Lorraine. I am in front of my cart with my back to her.

While standing there Lorraine suddenly does a running start with her cart, jumps on it and aims directly at me. I am unaware of this as my back is towards her. The shopping cart and Lorraine became the bowling ball and I was the pins. On impact I slid under the shopping cart and Lorraine fell to the floor. The associates in the store ran to the scene to assure we were okay and more importantly, to assure, that the store was not a target for litigation. But how can we file litigation when my silly cousin decided to play BJ & Lojo Bowling at midnight! As you can see sometimes just being near food makes you do the strangest things.

Family Memories

Salad Treasure

CULINARY ROOTS 35 BRENDA L. JACKSON

Salad Treasure

1 bag baby greens
1 thinly sliced medium Bermuda onion
1 can colossal olives pitted
1 can sliced beets
1 small bag carrot chips
2 rough cut medium tomatoes
1 can or jar of artichokes
1 avocado (sliced)
1 cup smoked gouda or Mexican cheese (cubed)
Balsamic vinaigrette dressing

- On a large platter place baby greens; creatively place remaining vegetables throughout the bed of baby greens; drizzle with vinaigrette.

- Makes a wonderful addition to parties, club meetings, etc.

Sausage Bacon Bites

Sausage Bacon Bites

1 pkg miniature sausages

12 oz pkg thinly sliced bacon

2 cups dark brown sugar

- Cut the bacon slices into thirds; wrap each piece of bacon around the sausage securing with a toothpick; repeat this step until sausage or bacon runs out; place brown sugar in container coat each wrapped sausage; then place on baking sheet.

- Preheat oven to 350 degrees; bake until bacon is crisp and sugar has caramelized.

- Not a fan of pork? Use turkey sausage and turkey bacon. This is a great appetizer to satisfy that salt & sweet craving.

Sausage Stew

Culinary Roots · 39 · Brenda L. Jackson

Sausage Stew

2 medium potatoes (rough cut w/skin on)

½ lb Andouille Cajun sausage

4 chorizo sausage (rough cut, remove casing)

1 medium onion chopped

1 medium sweet potato chopped

1 box frozen green peas

½ green bell pepper chopped

½ red bell pepper chopped

4 mini corn cobs cut in half

½ cup wild rice

6 cups chicken stock

1 tsp cinnamon

1 tsp allspice

1 tsp cumin

1 tsp pepper

1 tsp kosher salt

Dash red pepper

Olive oil

Sautee onion and garlic, adding sausages and browning; in a 4 quart pot add 6 cups of chicken stock; pour in chopped vegetables and seasonings. Bring to a boil; reduce heat and simmer for 50 minutes. Even better the second day.

Smothered Catfish

Smothered Catfish

4 medium size catfish (skinned without head)
complete seasoning
black pepper
hot sauce
flour
seasoned bread crumbs
1 onion (sliced)
3 tbsp olive oil
1 jar salsa (your preferred heat)
white wine

- Rinse fish thoroughly. Cut fish in half (across the the body of the fish). Score the fish at a slant. This allows for even frying. Season fish with black pepper, complete seasoning and hot sauce.

- In gallon size storage bag mix flour and seasoned bread crumbs (1 part flour to 2 parts bread crumbs). Coat fish with flour mixture.

- Fry in canola oil until golden brown.

Smother

Sauté onions in olive oil until translucent and slightly caramelized. Sprinkle 1 tbsp flour adding white wine and salsa. Stir gently over medium heat until thickened.
Place fish on platter and pour smother over fish and serve.

Steamed Tilapia W/ Sundried Tomatoes And Spinach

8 tilapia filets

Kosher salt, black pepper, garlic powder to taste

1 medium onion chopped

3 cloves garlic chopped

1/3 cup sundried tomatoes chopped

1 bag fresh spinach

½ can tomato sauce (seasoned with small pinches of pepper, cumin, kosher salt, cayenne pepper, cilantro, garlic powder)

1/2 cup white wine

3 tbsp olive oil

- Season fish with kosher salt, pepper and garlic set aside. Prepare tomato sauce mixture – set aside. Then sauté garlic and onion in olive oil until tender. Place seasoned filets on top and cover; cook on medium low until fish is steamed (flesh is white). Add spinach and sundried tomatoes. Add white wine and tomato sauce mixture. Simmer for 10 minutes or until spinach is wilted.

- Serve on a bed of rice or pasta.

Stewed Oxtails

Stewed Oxtails

2 lbs oxtails

½ cup flour

1 tsbp worcestershire

2 tsbp red wine

complete seasoning

black pepper

1 medium onion chopped

4 tbsp browning seasoning

2 tbsp olive oil

1 tbsp minced garlic (jar or tube)

2 tbsp butter

- Season oxtails with complete seasoning, black pepper, worcestershire; lightly flour oxtails; sauté minced garlic in 2 tbsp olive oil and butter; pan sear oxtails in fry pan for a brown crust on the meat. You are not trying to cook the meat here. When complete place in 4 quart pot; cover with water; add chopped onions and browning seasoning; allow pot to come to boil; reduce heat to medium heat and cook for 1 hour.

Sweet And Spicy Tuna Salad

Sweet and Spicy Tuna Salad

2 cans white albacore tuna packed in water

½ cup honey Dijon salad dressing

½ cup whipped salad dressing

½ tbsp yellow mustard

½ tsp celery seed

½ tsp paprika

Cajun seasoning for preferred heat

Seasoned pepper to taste

Balsamic vinaigrette dressing

- Drain tuna, combine with ingredients. Place tuna salad on a bed of baby greens (arugula); garnish with shredded carrots and sliced beets. Drizzle greens, carrots and beets with balsamic dressing.
- Serve with crackers or bagel chips.

Family Memories

With my father being adventurous in his cooking and having a twisted sense of humor, you had to be careful when asking what was cooking. Daddy loved to fabricate (pretty word) lie when responding to this question. When he said it was beef stew, it turned out to be stewed goat or other wild meat. By the time you get this information you have swallowed. Daddy would laugh hysterically at the wrenching and retching of our faces when it was too late to put the food back.

Needless to say, I inherited my father's sense of humor. My friends were over for dinner and I prepared a wonderful meal and everyone enjoyed it. When all were full and happy, I informed them they had just eaten fried turtle. You see, when I got the meat from my father, I prepared the turtle in the shape of a filet or medallion size. They were dredge in an egg, flour, Italian bread crumb batter and fried. Of course from that point I was intently scrutinized in the kitchen by my friends before they would eat my cooking again.

Teriyaki BBQ Turkey Wings

Teriyaki BBQ Turkey Wings

2-3 lbs turkey wings

(have the meat dept cut in pieces)

1 btl barbecue sauce

Marinade:

Half bottle teriyaki sauce

2 tsp white pepper

2 tsp ginger

1 tsp thyme

2 tsp garlic powder w/parsley

- Wash meat thoroughly. Pat dry with paper towel to remove moisture. Place turkey wings in a storage bag or a container with a cover. Pour marinade mixture on the turkey and let sit for an 1 hour or overnight.

- Preheat oven to 375 degrees. Place turkey parts in a roaster pan, cover with foil. Bake for 2 hours. Check for tenderness. Remove foil and pour barbecue sauce over turkey coating all the pieces. On low broil with the pan on the lower rack, broil for 10-15 minutes or until sauce has baked into the turkey and skin is crisping.

Vegetable Medley

Vegetable Medley

- 2 yellow squash
- 1 large zucchini
- 1 medium onion
- 2 garlic cloves
- 1 can stewed tomatoes
- Dash of red pepper flakes
- Complete seasonings
- Black pepper
- ½ cup white wine

- Slice squash and zucchini on an angle ¼ inch thick; slice onion and chop garlic then sauté in olive oil allowing onions to brown a little on the edges; add squash, zucchini and stewed tomatoes and white wine. Bring to a boil; reduce heat and let simmer for 20 minutes.

- Sprinkle with Parmesan or Romano Cheese and serve.

CULINARY ROOTS 55 BRENDA L. JACKSON

Wasabi Spinach Mashed Potatoes

Culinary Roots — 56 — Brenda L. Jackson

Wasabi Spinach Mashed Potatoes

2 lbs Yukon gold potatoes
1 box frozen chopped spinach
1 cup wasabi sauce (located in the ethnic aisle)
or sushi department of the grocery store)
1 can evaporated milk
Complete seasoning to taste
1 stick butter

- Rough cut potatoes leaving peel on and boil in salted water until tender; defrost spinach, squeeze out excess water.

- Thoroughly mash the potatoes adding butter, wasabi sauce and seasoning; add milk in parts to ensure mixture is not too soupy; fold in spinach.

Family Memories

The anticipation of reaching my grandmother's home in Gainesville would always bring a large smile to my face. Not just I, but all my brothers and sister would get ready for whatever dishes grandmother had prepared for our visit.

As much as we enjoyed all the various meals during the stay, leaving brought with it the same anticipation as did the arrival.
While the car was being loaded for departure, I always knew that the last item would be my grandmother's famous shoebox of goodies. You might think some cookies or cake. But no, in the box(es) would be fried chicken, perlo rice (rice prepared from homemade chicken stock), potato salad, cake and pies.

This made the long trip from Gainesville back home to Miami an eventful one! The simple shoebox(es) was always a culinary surprise and greatly enjoyed by all. I can taste it just in revisiting this moment. So as you can tell from the stories, the photos and the food, moments of love and joy was always a guaranteed result for my family.

Family Memories

Family Memories

While you have come towards the end of CULINARY ROOTS as a book - you are at the beginning of what I hope will be a wonderful return to building families with the wisdom of the kitchen and the communal table. Publisher E. Claudette Freeman shared with me how she loved going home to Pelham, Georgia as a little girl because she loved to wake up early and watch her grandmother cook. Does that sound like a familiar thing for you as well? Claudette says she would watch her grandmother slice ham, make biscuits and sometimes even bake cakes. She admits the flair for cooking was lost on her; instead, her favorite part of that time was simply listening to her grandmother talk about everything and anything and licking the bowl.

That is what happens when someone who loves her family and those around her through what she prepares in the kitchen really shines. I challenge you to pull from your family cooking and eating memories and create new ones unique to you. How? Well, two things come to mind...

COOKING CLUBS

A cooking club - are you kidding? Absolutely not! These could be awesome times of sharing wisdom, life, talking about the politics and economics of the day and of course cooking and eating.

Design your club according to your style or what you want to achieve. Your cooking club could be made up of family members only. Perhaps you are a cancer or other survivor and your cooking club will consist of those who have been amazing odds. A cool idea would be to have a generational cooking club, where your members are made up of more mature persons and teenagers or young adults.

Themes could be a great idea - you could go Mexican one meeting, Jamaican the next and even dabble in Indian or Moroccan cuisine. The possibilities are endless. Or your cooking club can go the SURPRISE route! Here is what I mean. Ask each member to brings one ingredient, they can not disclose what that ingredient is in advance. When the cooks gather on the evening (or day) of the meeting members present their individual ingredient contributions. Now the fun begins, because you have to figure out what palatable and edible dish can be created from the SURPRISE ingredients. Challenge yourself – try to prepare 2 dishes or even more and surprise yourself with your club's culinary skills.

Set your club up just like a book club. Choose meeting dates and locations - rotate kitchens if you want, even plan field trips to kitchens of restaurants you love. Decide how many members will add a nice flavor without spoiling the pot. Definitely pick a name that compliments what your club is all about: Hot Pepper Mama's, Cool and Collected Cooks, Boiling Babies.... or whatever it is all up to you.

COOKING COACHES

Totally re-invent yourself now that you have ignited or re-ignited your love for cooking and turn that passion into a part time hobby that can also produce revenue. Your clientele is vast - trust me. I do not think I clearly recognized how many of my friends can not cook or do not dare venture into anything fun in the kitchen out of fear. So I have decided that I am going to coach them into culinary success (or at least try) I sure hope my kitchen survives!

Fulfill your passion by seeking out your friends who cannot cook and/or family members that cannot cook (the take out containers are in the garbage can in the back yard and they have been fooling you.) Another great little clientele is youth who need to learn to cook – you could be the one that teaches them there is more to life than a burger or deli sandwich from a fast food restaurant.

Getting people in the kitchen and cooking (and loving it) is your focus. You can set your own schedule and set a small hourly rate. Hey, I know it seems like a far-fetched idea, same thing I thought - but I assure you it will be off when you see the one person that could not figure out how to boil water grinning widely, because they succeeded in making Honey Key Lime Chicken Wings. Social networking and back page community newspaper listings are a great way to find students; plus mass emails, blogging and word of mouth would be great marketing ideas.

Bon appetit and remember we have all had at least three disasters in the kitchen before we got it right.

BRENDA'S IDEAS FOR CULINARY ADVENTURES

1.   What can I do with pork chops to give them a new face?

It would be cool to stuff them with mashed sweet potatoes and glaze with cranberry sauce.

For stuffed pork chops purchase the center cut. Season the pork chops the way you like, slicing into the pork chop making a pocket; stuff with the mashed sweet potatoes (for How to see below).

Pan sear the chops on each side in olive oil. You are not cooking the meat to completion only to obtain a nice crust. Place chops in a shallow baking dish.

Preheat oven to 350. Bake for 45 minutes. Brush with cranberry glaze the last 15 minutes of baking.

Mashed Sweet Potatoes: You can either go fresh and peel and boil sweet potatoes or buy canned sweet potatoes, heat, mash adding butter, cinnamon, and nutmeg and please believe me – a little black pepper.

Cranberry Glaze: In a small pot simmer a can of cranberry sauce; for a kick add a little hot sauce.

2.   I am getting ready to cook for the first time for my honey. We were recently engaged and I want to do something that really says how much I appreciate him, what would you suggest?

Don't overtax yourself. You can obtain simplicity, elegance and romance in this 4-course meal. Make sure you serve in courses as the element of anticipation is sensual and romantic.

Quick Crab Tomato Bisque
Baby Green Salad w/Balsamic Vinaigrette
Chicken Penne Pasta w/Sundried Tomatoes
Mélange (fruit salad)

Soup: This is a simple task of buying already prepared condensed soups (cream of celery, clam chowder); a little half and half, cooking sherry or the real thing (I like the real thing) and then adding fresh crab and some tomato paste. Heat first, then puree in the blender and serve. The expensive part is the taste.

Salad: get a salad bag from the supermarket; any of the dark greens; a bottle of balsamic vinaigrette salad dressing. Do not mix salad until ready to serve.

Entrée: Prepare penne pasta according to directions on the box; purchase a roasted chicken (using the breast meat, remove skin and chop); sauté 1 tbsp minced garlic in 3 tbsp olive oil; add chicken and sundried tomatoes; pour in pink vodka pasta sauce and simmer for 10 minutes.

Dessert: It can be decadent, refreshing and believe it or not sexy. Pick up a fruit bowl at the market; pour your favorite sparkling wine (champagne, spumante) over the fruit to merry the flavor of the fruit with the wine. I make a mean mojito for mine. I would prepare this first, so when you are ready to serve, all the goodness of the fermented grape reaches its potential.

TIP OF THE NIGHT: Feed your man with a little sugar (smile) to the fruit – finger-fed foods are the best. ENJOY!!!

3. I am so tired of collard greens, turnip greens, mustard greens – is there anything that give them flavor besides fatty pork?

I like using smoked turkey in my greens and I also add a few cubes of chicken bouillon for flavor. If you are a fan of having a little heat in your food, throw in some scotch bonnet peppers, red pepper flakes and of course hot sauce. Remember to slow cook your greens – speed in today's world is overrated.

4. It's my turn to cook for the book club – what would you suggest as a great theme?

50's Diner Theme – serve a blue plate special (i.e. meatloaf w/gravy, mashed potatoes and green peas) for dessert - apple pie ala mode; cherry coke (add a little rum if you like);

Same theme making menu a little more casual: burgers, fries and malts or milkshakes (add a little rum if you like).

5. I absolutely love tilapia. Give me some great ideas to make it hot and interesting every time I cook it.
Here are a few suggestions:

- Steamed tilapia in onions, garlic, ginger and celery
- Baked/Broil tilapia seasoned with lime, grill seasoning and honey – bake for 10 minutes; broil for 5 minutes.

Also change the accompaniment (side dish). Place on a bed of pasta; mango salsa; or even spinach mashed potatoes.

6. The other day I must have stood in the vegetable section for an hour; trying to figure out what I could do with spinach and broccoli to really enjoy them. Finally, I decided on a chocolate cake and left. What ideas do you have to help me like these two vegetables better?

Spinach and broccoli are enjoyable raw or cooked. Served as a salad, rice dish, in pasta primavera, in soups, chicken broccoli rice casserole, spinach tomato mozzarella appetizer; spinach and ricotta cheese wrapped and baked in filo (thin pastry); mashed potatoes; cold pasta salad; broccoli cheese bake.

While doing a four-week detox program, I even found this great and oh so quick Italian bean soup (sauté onion and garlic in olive oil, add in a can of white lima beans or any white bean and spinach; cover and cook on medium for 5 minutes).
Be creative wherever you use the spinach interchange with the broccoli.

7. I have to bring the cornbread for the family dinner next week. My goal is to do something that will even impress my grandmother, any ideas?

You can never go wrong with baking with sour cream when preparing a dish to impress the matriarchs of the family. Get creative in the kitchen take the smells of the kitchen during the holidays and put that in your cornbread. Think of the flavors you love in your turkey dressing/stuffing (i.e. sausage, onions, sage, etc.). The memories of those smells can only enhance the ambiance of the dinner table. Enjoy the compliments to come!

8. My husband and I want to plan an indoor picnic (our last two rained out) for about 10 friends – any menu options that are unusual but easy and what would suggest for the table design?

Honey Key Lime Chicken Wings – these are cooked in the oven and then broiled for a few minutes after placing the honey. The secret to this is marinating in seasoning and fresh lime overnight.

Layered Salad – build a salad in layers of your favorite vegetables – tasty and decorative.

Fruit salad kabobs – add Malibu rum to already prepared fruit salad, let marinate and then place on skewers.

This menu is tasty, decorative, easy serve, easy cleanup.

Make your tablescape a Key West theme (Buffet style): Use palm fronds as chargers to hold the platters of food; cylinder candles of ocean blue green, white and taupe; place conch shells and seashells throughout the table. Use plates, cups, cutlery and napkins that theme appropriate in color or design.

OTHER TITLES FROM

PECAN TREE PUBLISHING, INC

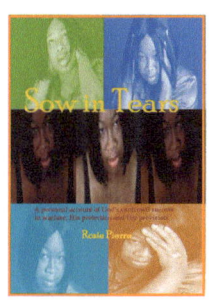

Sow in Tears
By Rosie Pierre

The Morning Hour
By E. Claudette Freeman

PARABLES
The bi-monthly Journal
of Christian short-fiction
and devotionals

www.ingramcontent.com/pod-product-compliance
Lightning Source LLC
Chambersburg PA
CBHW042024150426
43198CB00002B/54